Original title:
The Fading Horizon

Copyright © 2024 Creative Arts Management OÜ
All rights reserved.

Author: Alec Donovan
ISBN HARDBACK: 978-9916-88-890-2
ISBN PAPERBACK: 978-9916-88-891-9

The Breath Between Light and Dark

In twilight's hush, the shadows creep,
A gentle sigh where secrets sleep.
The sun dips low, its warmth fades fast,
A fleeting moment, too brief to last.

The stars emerge, a whispered call,
Painting the night, enchanting all.
In every pause, a story told,
Of dreams that shimmer, brave and bold.

Whispers Beneath the Stars

Under the vast, eternal sky,
Soft voices murmur, a lullaby.
Each twinkling light, a tale to share,
Of distant worlds and secrets rare.

Beneath the moon, shadows play,
Dancing softly, night turns to day.
In silence deep, our hopes take flight,
They weave through dreams, igniting light.

Glowing Remnants of a Day Unlived

The sun once bright, now a memory faint,
A canvas brushed with hues of paint.
In every corner, echoes reside,
Of laughter shared, of joy and pride.

Yet time's embrace holds moments tight,
Some dreams unfurl, while others might.
A whispered wish on the evening breeze,
Flickering softly through swaying trees.

Between Two Realms

Where twilight meets the edge of night,
A world unfolds, both dark and bright.
Step lightly on this fragile line,
Where shadows linger, hearts entwine.

In this space where silence reigns,
The whispers of old love still pains.
Here time stands still, a sacred trust,
In the realms of dreams, we find ourmust.

Departing Hues

Colors of twilight softly blend,
Whispers of night on every bend.
Orange and violet dance the sky,
As daylight bids a slow goodbye.

Fading light begins to wane,
Echoes of laughter, joy, and pain.
Stars awaken, shyly they peek,
In the silence, the world feels meek.

Fade into the Abyss

Shadows crawl as the light moves away,
Holding secrets of the waning day.
Time drips slowly like melting wax,
In the silence, the heart relax.

Thoughts dissolve into a quiet stream,
Lost in darkness, chasing a dream.
Whispers beckon from the unknown,
Guided by echoes, we're never alone.

The Velvet Cloak of Dusk

Wrapped in warmth of twilight's grace,
Stars emerge in their tender place.
Veils of dusk with a gentle hand,
Brush the world, as dreams expand.

Softly the night begins to hum,
Crickets whisper where shadows come.
Every heartbeat is a fleeting spark,
Guiding us through the enveloping dark.

Memories of a Brilliant Day

Sunshine smiles on fields of gold,
Stories of summer, waiting to be told.
Laughter echoes in vibrant hues,
Crafting moments we can't lose.

As twilight falls, those gems remain,
Cascading warmth, soft like rain.
In our hearts, they light the way,
Bringing joy to grayest day.

The Last Brush of Daylight

The sun dips low, a golden hue,
Painting the sky in shades so new.
Whispers of dusk begin to call,
As shadows stretch and softly fall.

Colors blend, a fleeting dance,
Nature holds its breath, entranced.
Birds retreat to nests so tight,
Embracing the calm of coming night.

Glimmering Solitude at Sunset

In silence, the world slows to a gleam,
The horizon blushes, a waking dream.
Waves of twilight wash ashore,
Every heartbeat whispers, 'Want more'.

Alone in beauty, a fleeting breath,
Where daylight fades, begins the quest.
Stars emerge in velvet skies,
Gentle secrets, ancient sighs.

Slow Embrace of the Night

The twilight lingers, soft and deep,
As shadows stir from fitting sleep.
Night unfolds her tender arms,
Wrapping the world in calming charms.

Moonlight filters through the trees,
A serenade upon the breeze.
Each star twinkles with quiet grace,
In the vastness, we find our place.

A Soft Descent

The day concedes to night's embrace,
A gentle shift, a whispered pace.
With each breath, the calm descends,
As nature sleeps, the world mends.

Softly now, the shadows weave,
A tapestry that few perceive.
In the darkness, dreams ignite,
Softening the edges of the night.

Whispers of an Evening Breeze

Gentle winds caress the trees,
Carrying secrets of the seas.
Stars flicker in the fading light,
As day surrenders to the night.

Crickets sing their evening song,
In harmony where we belong.
Moonlight dances on the ground,
In these whispers, peace is found.

Melodies of a Dying Radiance

Sunset paints the world in gold,
A tale of warmth, quietly told.
Colors blend in a soft embrace,
As night begins to take its place.

The last light shimmers on the lake,
A fleeting moment, hearts awake.
In this beauty, time stands still,
Melodies echo, sweet and shrill.

The Final Fade-Out

Shadows stretch across the land,
In silence, we take a stand.
Memories linger in the air,
As whispers weave a tale so rare.

With every breath, a soft goodbye,
As stars emerge in the dark sky.
The clock ticks softly, drawing near,
The final fade-out, bittersweet year.

Twilight's Final Offering

Twilight drapes a velvet shawl,
Enveloping the world, so small.
In shades of blue and hints of grey,
The sun waves softly, fades away.

A hush descends on every street,
Where shadows blend, and dreamers meet.
In this calm, we find our place,
Twilight's gift, an embrace of grace.

The Edge of Diverging Paths

At the fork in the dim light,
Choices glimmer, shadows dance,
Left or right, what feels right?
Heart whispers, take a chance.

One road leads to the unknown,
Silent echoes fill the air,
The other smiles, warmly grown,
Comfort cradles me with care.

Each step weighs the dreams I chase,
Footprints linger, fading fast,
In their depth, I search for grace,
Unraveled thoughts of future past.

Yet the path less traveled winds,
Through thickets thick, and fears abound,
A journey waits where hope unwinds,
Embracing all that can be found.

Vanishing Luminescence

Softly fades the evening glow,
Stars awaken, one by one,
In the hush, the night will show,
Whispers of a day now done.

Fragments of a light once bright,
Dance upon the velvet sea,
But the dawn, with its first light,
Promises the end of glee.

Shadows stretch where dreams had played,
Silhouettes of what was dear,
Memories, like wisps, cascade,
Into realms of fleeting cheer.

Letting go of what has passed,
Relinquish time, let it flow,
For in night's embrace, I cast,
Tender thoughts of long ago.

Twilight's Gentle Lullaby

As the sun bids soft goodbye,
Whispers blend with twilight's sigh,
Nature hums a tender tune,
Crickets play their sweet maroon.

Purple hues touch the distant hills,
Stars awaken with silken thrills,
A gentle breeze caresses leaves,
In this magic, the heart believes.

Softly comes the night's embrace,
Wrapping all in stillness' grace,
Dreams are woven in this light,
Cradled close amidst the night.

In twilight's arms, I find my rest,
Lost in peace, I am my best,
With each note, a soul's release,
In night's cradle, I find peace.

The Unraveling Sky

Gray clouds gather, darkness swells,
A tempest brews with whispered spells,
Tides of fate, they rise and fall,
The sky's canvas, breathing all.

Lightning strikes, a fleeting flash,
Illuminates the storm's loud crash,
Rain cascades like silver tears,
Washing dreams, dissolving fears.

Above, a tapestry unwinds,
Secrets lost in swirling winds,
A horizon, torn and frayed,
Yet within chaos, hope is laid.

When the storm shall cease to roar,
And the sun breaks through once more,
I will stand 'neath skies anew,
Embracing all the bright and blue.

Last Glimmer of Hope

In shadows deep, where sorrows tread,
A flicker shines, a heart unled.
Through darkness thick, one light remains,
Soft whispers call, break through the chains.

With every tear, a lesson learned,
From ashes cold, a spirit burned.
Embrace the dawn, for night must fade,
A new path waits, be not afraid.

A Sky in Retreat

The clouds roll in, a silent shroud,
Once bright and bold, now lost, unbowed.
The sun dips low, in shades of gray,
While twilight sings, the night to play.

Stars begin to blink and tease,
Whispers ride upon the breeze.
A sky that fades, reveals the night,
In darkened hues, awaits the light.

Embers of Evening

The fire softens, embers glow,
A fading warmth within the flow.
The twilight whispers, tales untold,
In colors rich, both bright and bold.

The day surrenders, bids adieu,
As night descends, a tranquil hue.
With every spark, a memory plays,
In embers glint, the past still stays.

Secrets Beneath the Sundown

When day concedes to evening's grace,
The shadows dance, they find their place.
Hidden truths in whispers wind,
Revealing what the dark can find.

The sun descends, a curtain drawn,
In hushed tones, the night is born.
With every star, a secret shared,
Beneath the sky, souls unpaired.

Fading Dreams on the Edge

Whispers of dawn kiss the night,
Fading visions lose their light.
Shadows dance in gentle sway,
As hope drifts slowly away.

In corners where silence dwells,
Old memories cast their spells.
Fleeting moments, lost in air,
Echoes linger, light as prayer.

Once vibrant, now shades of gray,
Dreams, they falter, drift astray.
Softly sighing, they dissolve,
In the abyss, they revolve.

Yet in the dusk, new dreams take form,
From the ashes, they will warm.
A promise born on the edge,
Where faded dreams dare to pledge.

Colors That Whisper Goodbye

Crimson skies as day departs,
Brush of gold, it stings the hearts.
Whispers linger on the breeze,
Tales of joy and soft unease.

Azure thoughts drift out of reach,
Lessons learned, the past to teach.
Emerald glimmers fade away,
In twilight's arms, they gently sway.

Violet shadows stretch and blend,
Colors fade, the world transcends.
A canvas painted with the sighs,
Of fleeting moments, soft goodbyes.

Beneath the hues, memories bide,
Emotions wrapped in colors wide.
They softly whisper, fall like tears,
As the twilight calms our fears.

Silhouettes Against a Dimming Sky

Figures stand where dreams collide,
Against the dusk, they stretch and glide.
Shapes of hope, yet shadows tall,
In the twilight, they enthrall.

With every breath, the night unfolds,
Stories whispered, gently told.
Fleeting moments, lost in time,
Echo softly, pure as rhyme.

As the sun sinks, hearts align,
In silhouettes, the stars define.
Night will cradle all that's dear,
Casting shadows, drawing near.

Hold the silence, let it play,
Underneath this dimming sway.
In darkened hues, we'll find our way,
Silhouettes against the gray.

The Horizon's Quiet Farewell

In silence, the horizon sighs,
A gentle kiss from tender skies.
With every hue that fades to black,
A promise sent, no turning back.

Waves of twilight brush the shore,
Whispers echo, tales of yore.
The sun bows low, as if to grieve,
For moments lost, we can't retrieve.

Stars awaken, one by one,
Guiding thoughts till night is done.
In this hush, a truth prevails,
In quietude, the heart exhales.

As shadows stretch and dreams take flight,
The horizon holds the fleeting light.
With every farewell, we embrace,
The promise of another place.

Approaching the Dark Verge

The sun dips low in the sky,
Casting shadows long and shy.
Whispers chill the evening air,
As night creeps in without a care.

Stars begin to blink awake,
While the moon starts to break.
A tapestry of night unspools,
Revealing ancient, hidden jewels.

The trees sway soft in twilight's embrace,
As shadows dance, a ghostly race.
Each breeze carries a haunting song,
A reminder that night won't be long.

Underneath the vast dark dome,
All creatures settle, finding home.
Silence falls, a precious gift,
As the world begins to shift.

Beyond the Last Ray

Beyond the last ray of light,
The world holds its breath in night.
Mysteries begin to weave,
Whispers of what we dare believe.

Flickering dreams paint the dark,
A canvas where shadows embark.
Crickets play their serenade,
As night descends, secrets invade.

Every heartbeat resonates slow,
In the deep where few ever go.
The horizon blurs into a haze,
Caught in twilight's gentle phase.

Perhaps there lies a silver line,
Where dreams and reality intertwine.
Lost in wonder, the night unfolds,
Telling tales the moon beholds.

Whispers of Dusk

Whispers of dusk lightly call,
As colors fade, surrendering all.
Gentle hues of pink and grey,
Child of twilight, come what may.

The horizon softens, peace descends,
In silence where the day transcends.
Soft sighs echo through the trees,
As the world bends with evening's breeze.

A realm where shadows play their part,
Hiding secrets in the heart.
With every step, the darkness hums,
A melody of distant drums.

Here the stars begin to bloom,
Dancing free within the gloom.
Each twinkle holds a fleeting dream,
In the quiet, hope's gentle beam.

Echoes of Dimming Light

Echoes of dimming light depart,
Gently wrapping night's warm heart.
The last glow starts to wane,
Revealing softly the evening's reign.

Each shadow grows, a silent friend,
As day surrenders, bidding end.
Street lamps flicker, a golden sheen,
Illuminating the spaces in between.

Night unfolds its heavy cloak,
With whispered tales that softly stoke.
Memories drift upon the breeze,
Carried far on hushed unease.

In the stillness, dreams arise,
Dancing softly 'neath muted skies.
Each heartbeat echoes through the night,
A pulse of magic, pure delight.

Night's Gentle Unraveling

The stars begin to gleam,
As shadows softly creep,
The world slips into dreams,
In silence, secrets keep.

The moon hangs in the sky,
A guardian of the night,
Whispers of a lullaby,
As day surrenders light.

Soft breezes start to play,
Through leaves that gently sway,
The darkness holds its sway,
In night's embrace, we stay.

With each tick of the clock,
A moment slowly fades,
While time begins to dock,
In evening's cool cascades.

The Horizon's Last Caress

The sun dips low and slow,
Its colors paint the skies,
A fiery, golden glow,
As daylight softly dies.

Waves kiss the sandy shore,
In rhythm, they retreat,
The horizon seeks for more,
In dance with dusk, so sweet.

Clouds blush in pink and gold,
A fleeting, warm embrace,
The day's last story told,
In twilight's calm embrace.

As night begins to reign,
The stars emerge with pride,
In beauty, yet again,
The day becomes a guide.

The Edge of Dusk

Between the day and night,
A whisper fills the air,
A moment pure delight,
As sunlight learns to share.

The shadows grow and twine,
With hues of deepening blue,
The world, a painted line,
Where day bids night adieu.

Birds sing their last refrain,
As crickets start their song,
The calm begins to reign,
In dusk where dreams belong.

A fleeting breath of peace,
In colors richly swirled,
As twilight's touch will cease,
A promise of the world.

Cradled by Twilight

The sky turns soft and gray,
As daylight starts to fade,
The colors drift away,
In twilight's gentle shade.

A hush wraps all around,
The world begins to slow,
In moments yet unbound,
Where secrets start to grow.

The stars take up their posts,
As night begins to hum,
With whispers, tender ghosts,
To soothe where shadows come.

Cradled in evening's bliss,
Our worries drift away,
In twilight's sweet abyss,
We find a place to stay.

Hues of a Dying Day

The sun dips low, a fiery hue,
Across the sky, a canvas new.
Whispers of gold, soft and slow,
As night creeps in, with gentle glow.

Shadows stretch and colors fade,
In this fleeting masquerade.
Crimson embers, a final call,
Nature sighs, awaiting fall.

Beneath the arch of twilight's grace,
Old memories in colors trace.
Each stroke of dusk, a painted sigh,
As stars awaken in the sky.

The world stands still as if to pray,
In the hues of this dying day.
Each moment lingers, soft and bright,
In the embrace of coming night.

Beyond the Vanishing Edge

Where the sea meets the sky's embrace,
A horizon lost, an endless race.
Waves of whispers, secrets spun,
Beneath the glow of a setting sun.

Clouds dance softly, a fading dream,
On the edge of time, they gleam.
Ripples echo, as thoughts collide,
Beyond that line, hope cannot hide.

The world extends, but dreams confine,
Navigating paths, both yours and mine.
In the twilight's breath, we seek the pledge,
Of what lies soft, beyond the edge.

Hold your breath, let shadows blend,
In the dusk, where time might bend.
With every step, a wish we send,
Beyond the vanishing's gentle end.

The Last Sigh of Day

As evening cloaks the world in peace,
The last sigh drifts, a sweet release.
Echoes linger, soft and bold,
In twilight's arms, as stories unfold.

Stars awaken, a twinkling cheer,
With the night, they draw us near.
In whispered tones, the shadows play,
Reflecting dreams from the day.

The moon spills silver on the ground,
In this hallowed hush, we are bound.
Each breath of night holds memories tight,
In the fabric woven of starlight.

Await the dawn, but cherish now,
This fleeting hour, we'll take a bow.
For in the dark, our hopes shall sway,
As we breathe in the last sigh of day.

Memories in Softening Colors

In a palette rich, our memories sing,
Softening colors that life can bring.
Each hue a story, each shade a heart,
A painting crafted, a work of art.

Faded roses, whispers of time,
In sepia tones, life's sweet rhyme.
Brush strokes gentle, as voices blend,
Across the canvas, paths extend.

Golden glimmers of laughter's share,
Silhouettes dance in the evening air.
With every shade, a cherished glance,
In the twilight glow, we find romance.

So hold onto these colors, bold yet tender,
In the softening light, let's remember.
For in each moment, love takes flight,
In memories wrapped in hues of light.

In the Arms of Dusk

Whispers soft as fading light,
Embraced in hues of gentle night.
The shadows dance, the sky ignites,
In the arms of dusk, life takes flight.

Crickets sing a lullaby,
As daylight bids its sweet goodbye.
A canvas draped in colors rare,
In twilight's glow, we shed our care.

Stars awaken one by one,
As the world finds peace, undone.
In twilight's grip, we fade away,
In the arms of dusk, we choose to stay.

Lullabies of Dimming Stars

Softly hum the stars above,
Melodies of peace and love.
Each twinkle tells a tale so deep,
In lullabies, the cosmos sleeps.

Gentle breezes carry sighs,
From dreamers looking to the skies.
The night unfolds its velvet dome,
In this embrace, we find our home.

Shimmers dim, yet hearts ignite,
In the hush of fading light.
With every flicker, dreams take flight,
In lullabies of dimming stars, we delight.

Nightfall's Tender Heart

Nightfall has a tender heart,
Wrapped in shadows, worlds depart.
The moonlit whispers weave and bind,
In gentle arms, we seek and find.

Underneath a blanket dark,
Every silence leaves a mark.
While time pauses, spirits rise,
In nightfall's gleam, we blend the skies.

Embrace the calm, the cool, the sweet,
Where dreams and waking lives do meet.
With every breath, we play our part,
In the glow of nightfall's tender heart.

A Brush of Dusk

A brush of dusk paints skies anew,
With strokes of purple, gold, and blue.
The day exhales a soothing breath,
As shadows whisper tales of death.

Clouds wear crowns of twilight's glow,
Nature's canvas put on show.
While time slips gently, unconfined,
A brush of dusk, we are entwined.

Every corner hugs the night,
With sparks of stars, a dazzling sight.
In this soft embrace, we find,
A brush of dusk, our hearts unlined.

When Colors Begin to Weep

When colors begin to weep,
The sky sheds its vibrant hues,
Whispers of twilight softly creep,
In silence, the world renews.

The red turns to shades of gray,
A canvas kissed by the breeze,
Memories fade, drift away,
As daylight bows with soft ease.

Clouds gather, heavy with thought,
As twilight holds its gentle hand,
In the weeping, solace is sought,
Colors bleed across the land.

In the hush of this vibrant night,
Stars awaken, one by one,
Drifting in the soft twilight,
As the colors begin to run.

Beneath the Twilight Veil

Beneath the twilight veil we stand,
Where shadows dance on the ground,
A hush falls softly over the land,
As crickets sing their gentle sound.

The sky blushes in muted tones,
Whispers linger on the breeze,
Every heartbeat, a world alone,
In the twilight's tender freeze.

Misty dreams weave through the trees,
Night unveils her secret charms,
With every sigh, the heart agrees,
Beneath her spell, our spirit warms.

Stars appear, like sparkles light,
A symphony of whispered grace,
In the embrace of coming night,
We find our still, enchanted place.

Night's Quieting Song

Night whispers a quiet song,
As shadows waltz with the moon,
In this moment, we belong,
To the rhythm of a soft tune.

In every rustle of the leaves,
The melody wraps around,
A gentle hush that gently weaves,
In the silence, peace is found.

Stars twinkle in perfect array,
A choir of lights far above,
Guiding lost souls on their way,
In the dark, we find our love.

With each note, the world slows down,
As night holds us, calm and near,
In this serenade of the town,
We listen close, we hear, we cheer.

Horizons Never to Return

Horizons stretch like endless dreams,
Where the sky meets the depth of sea,
A canvas brushed with soft moonbeams,
In quiet, hope flows wild and free.

The sunset bleeds its final light,
Waves whisper tales from afar,
As day gives way to the embracing night,
Sailing beneath a guiding star.

Each moment lost to time's sweet hold,
Lingers in echoes of the day,
Stories of journeys yet untold,
Covered in twilight's gentle sway.

In this realm where shadows live,
Horizons call, yet never return,
For every sunset, moments give,
And in their glow, our hearts still burn.

Celestial Beginnings of Endings

Stars awaken in the dusk,
Painting whispers in the sky,
Each twinkle tells a story,
Of dreams that never die.

The moonstone glimmers softly,
Casting shadows on the ground,
While twilight wraps the world,
In a tapestry profound.

A journey starts where light fades,
Embracing night's gentle breath,
Every ending births a start,
A dance of life and death.

In the stillness, hearts will soar,
To the rhythm of the night,
Celestial beginnings rise,
In the silence, pure delight.

Fragments of a Dying Day

Colors bleed across the sky,
As the sun bows down to rest,
Each hue a fleeting memory,
In the evening's peaceful quest.

Clouds drift like whispers soft,
Carrying tales of the bright,
While shadows stretch and linger,
Bringing forth the calming night.

Birds sing their last sweet chords,
In the twilight's gentle grasp,
Their melodies fade and swell,
As the daylight starts to clasps.

Fragments of a dying day,
Nestled in the night's embrace,
Tomorrow's hopes await the dawn,
In this still and sacred space.

Canvas of Nightfall

The canvas stretches overhead,
Brushed with hues of deepening blue,
Stars are splattered in silver glints,
As darkness breathes a life anew.

A quiet hush descends like dew,
Wrapping the world in velvet calm,
Nature sighs in soft repose,
While night sings her soothing psalm.

Moonlight spills upon the earth,
Turning shadows into dreams,
Every ripple of the night,
Holds a world of silent themes.

In this cosmic artwork spun,
Life pauses to admire grace,
A canvas of nightfall bright,
Where hope finds its gentle place.

Reflections in the Dimming Glow

As the light begins to fade,
Reflections dance upon the lake,
Each ripple holds a memory,
Of moments lost, a heart at stake.

The failing sun dips low and shy,
Kissing the horizon's edge,
While whispers carry through the trees,
In a twilight, soft and dredged.

Glimmers of a world unseen,
Sprinkle magic on the waves,
Where silence speaks in melodies,
Of the past and all it saves.

Reflections in the dimming glow,
Invite us to pause, reflect,
In the fading light of day,
Find solace in what we protect.

The Last Faint Glow

In twilight's soft embrace, we stand,
A whisper of the day so grand.
The horizon fades to shades of gray,
Where sunlight kisses night away.

The Last Faint Glow

A flicker glimmers by the trees,
As shadows sway in evening breeze.
The stars begin their gentle rise,
To greet the moonlit velvet skies.

The Last Faint Glow

The world slows down, the colors blend,
While night encroaches, day must end.
Yet in this pause, a beauty glows,
In every heart, the warmth still flows.

The Last Faint Glow

So let us linger, take it in,
This fleeting light, where dreams begin.
For even as the shadows grow,
We cherish here, the last faint glow.

Reflections on the Vanishing Light

As day departs with whispered sighs,
The sun sinks low, beneath the skies.
Each ray that fades, a tale untold,
In colors bold, and shadows old.

Reflections on the Vanishing Light

Mirrors of dusk brush past our eyes,
We watch the time in silence fly.
The earth transforms, so still, so bright,
A canvas stretched by fading light.

Reflections on the Vanishing Light

The sunset drips like honey slow,
On quiet lakes, soft ripples flow.
Each reflection tells us to unwind,
Embrace the moment, still, unconfined.

Reflections on the Vanishing Light

For in this dance of dark and bright,
We find the magic in the night.
And though the light may fade from sight,
Its memory lingers, pure delight.

A Dance with Shadows

In the hush of eve, shadows creep,
Where secrets dwell and silence keeps.
We sway beneath the twilight's glow,
As whispers of the night bestow.

A Dance with Shadows

In the moon's soft light we twist and turn,
With every flicker, our spirits yearn.
Each shadow tells a story spun,
Of battles lost and dreams we've won.

A Dance with Shadows

We find our rhythm in the dark,
The music flows, igniting spark.
A blend of hearts, a bond so rare,
We lose ourselves in midnight's care.

A Dance with Shadows

So let us twirl 'neath starlit skies,
Where shadows dance and memories rise.
In every step, a tale we weave,
In this embrace, we shall believe.

The Sky's Gentle Farewell

The sun dips low with soft goodbyes,
As dreams unfold in amber skies.
A palette rich, a fleeting show,
Beneath the arch of evening's glow.

The Sky's Gentle Farewell

Each cloud absorbs the colors bright,
Painting horizons with fading light.
In quiet awe, we watch and sigh,
As daylight whispers, 'Time to fly.'

The Sky's Gentle Farewell

With every shade of warmth it lends,
A promise keeps, though daylight ends.
In twilight's arms, we find our peace,
And in the stillness, moments cease.

The Sky's Gentle Farewell

As night unfurls its starry quilt,
We gather memories the day has built.
In every breath, a wish we send,
For all goodbyes, there's love to mend.

Journey into the Gloaming

The sun dips low, a fading crown,
Shadows stretch, they gently drown.
Whispers weave through twilight air,
As night unfolds its velvet stare.

Footsteps soft on winding trails,
With each breath, the daylight pales.
Stars awaken, one by one,
Marking where the journey's spun.

In the hush of dusk's embrace,
Lost in time, we find our place.
Every heartbeat, every sigh,
Threads of dusk that never die.

A canvas painted deep and wide,
Where secrets and the shadows hide.
In gloaming's grip, we dance and sway,
A timeless tale, we drift away.

A Soliloquy at Sundown

Beneath the sky, a stage is set,
The sun rehearses its grand exit.
Silhouettes in gold and gray,
Speak of dreams that fade away.

In this moment, hearts exposed,
The weight of day has now opposed.
Words of wonder, soft and low,
A soliloquy in twilight's glow.

Nature listens, crickets sing,
As shadows stretch, the night takes wing.
Memory dances in the light,
A fleeting glimpse, a whispered night.

With dimming rays, reflections stir,
In every thought, a gentle blur.
The curtain falls on sunlit skies,
As night unveils its starry guise.

When Light Begins to Weep

When light begins to weep and fade,
The vibrant colors slowly wade.
A soft embrace, the shadows creep,
And all the world begins to sleep.

Each ray a tear, a whispered sigh,
As dusk descends from skies up high.
In this hour, all dreams take flight,
Painting hopes in shades of night.

The silence hums, the air is still,
As hearts awaken, time to fill.
With secrets spun in fibers deep,
We hold our breath, our promise keep.

A canvas drawn with dusk's embrace,
Where time and space begin to trace.
In twilight's arms, we find our way,
When light begins to softly sway.

The Quiet Unraveling

In softest hues, the evening glides,
As day and night entwine their tides.
The world unveils its hidden seams,
Threaded through our quiet dreams.

With every breath, the fabric frays,
Embers of light in gentle plays.
A whisper here, a sighing breeze,
Nature's song, a tender tease.

In shadows deep, our spirits rise,
Unraveled hopes beneath the skies.
The heartbeats sync, a tranquil beat,
As dusk descends, we find our seat.

In this stillness, all is known,
Each fleeting moment, brightly sown.
The quiet winds their secrets share,
Unraveling time, beyond compare.

Hushed Goodbyes

In twilight's breath, we part,
Silent echoes in the heart.
Footsteps fade on gravel paths,
Leaving whispers, quiet laughs.

Eyes that linger, stories told,
Embers glowing, moments bold.
Time drifts softly, shadows blend,
In the hush, we find our end.

The moon shines bright, a silver friend,
As we embrace the night to mend.
Distance stretches, yet feels close,
In goodbyes, love's fragrance grows.

So let the stars be our guide,
In the night, we will abide.
With hopes entwined, let dreams arise,
In every heart, our whispered ties.

The Dimming Spectacle

The sun bows low, a curtain drawn,
As colors bleed, the day is gone.
Crimson skies and amber hues,
Paint the world with soft adieu.

Birds take flight, wings spread wide,
Chasing shadows, homeward glide.
In fading light, the whispers play,
Of dreams fulfilled, of lost array.

The stars emerge, like scattered lace,
In twilight's arms, we find our place.
As darkness drapes the earth anew,
A canvas born of deeper blue.

Each moment lingers, time stands still,
As night descends with quiet thrill.
The spectacle dims, yet hearts ignite,
In the dance of day, in the waltz of night.

Traces of Gold on Dusk's Canvas

The horizon blushes, gold unfurls,
Soft gentle tints that light the swirls.
Each brushstroke whispers tales so old,
Of sunlit dreams and secrets bold.

In the fading light, shadows play,
Fleeting moments slip away.
Yet in the dusk, we find our thread,
Connections linger, gently spread.

Clouds embrace the day's last breath,
A golden farewell, a gentle rest.
While darkness wraps the world in shrouds,
We paint with hope upon the clouds.

Each trace of gold, a memory's gift,
In the twilight's glow, our spirits lift.
As night unfolds its velvet hue,
We hold the sparks of dreams anew.

When Light Becomes Memory

When morning breaks and shadows flee,
Light spills out, a tapestry.
But time, it flows like running streams,
Carving out our buried dreams.

Moments flicker, a candle's glow,
Remnants here and there to show.
In the soft embrace of memory's hold,
We find ourselves in stories told.

As daylight fades, the echoes start,
Whispers linger in the heart.
Each ray a story, a time embraced,
In memories kept, we find our place.

So let the light become the past,
In gentle waves, a love that lasts.
When light becomes memory's song,
In the heart, it will belong.

Whispers of Dimming Light

In the hush of fading day,
Soft secrets find their way.
Stars begin to softly gleam,
As night unfolds its gentle dream.

Silhouettes in twilight's grace,
Wanderers in a quiet space.
Threads of gold in slackened skies,
Whispered truths in silent sighs.

The world slows in a tender pause,
Wrapped in nature's soothing cause.
With every rustle, shadows weave,
A tapestry of hopes believed.

With dusk's kiss on the moor,
Hearts begin to softly soar.
Through shadows, light begins to dart,
In whispered tales, we find our heart.

Shadows at Dusk

Beneath the arch of twilight blue,
Shadows stretch, revealing true.
Figures dance in muted light,
Chasing whispers into night.

Rustling leaves, a gentle tune,
Calling forth the crescent moon.
Echoing in quiet refrain,
The solace found in softest rain.

Footsteps linger on the path,
Caught in evening's warm embrace.
Time slows with each fleeting breath,
Every moment, a quiet depth.

As dusk swathes the land anew,
Shadows blend with dreams we view.
In the cradle of the night,
We find our peace in whispered light.

Echoes of Distant Dreams

In the silence of the night,
Echoes dance, out of sight.
Softly calling, hearts will leap,
In the whispers, secrets keep.

Fleeting visions, memory's flight,
Woven in the fabric of light.
Moments trapped in twilight's hush,
Where dreams are born in a gentle rush.

The stars align, a guiding spark,
Navigating through the dark.
Each shimmer holds a story clear,
Where distant dreams draw ever near.

With each echo, hopes ignite,
Carried forth by wings of night.
In the realm where shadows blend,
We find the paths that never end.

Twilight's Embrace

As day softly yields to night,
Twilight drapes the world in light.
A gentle hush falls from the sky,
In the calm where stillness lies.

Colors merge in splendid grace,
Nature wraps the stars' embrace.
Every breath a promise made,
In the twilight's grand parade.

Cascading whispers in the trees,
Dance upon the evening breeze.
Each heartbeat finds a place to rest,
In this moment, we are blessed.

Forever caught in dusk's design,
A fleeting glimpse of the divine.
In twilight's arms, we dream again,
Finding paths where love will reign.

Shadows of an Expiring Day

Shadows stretch in golden hues,
Whispers of the day lose their muse.
Leaves rustle softly as they sway,
Time paints the world in shades of gray.

The sun dips low, its warmth still near,
While twilight brings a hint of fear.
Minutes fade, a fleeting play,
As dusk creeps in, with dreams at bay.

The Fraying Edges of Light

Edges fray as colors blend,
The light begins its gentle end.
Crickets chirp, the calls cicada,
Nature hums a soft serenade.

Golden rays now softly fade,
Into a hush, a twilight shade.
Chasing stars that start to gleam,
Night awakes from daylight's dream.

Silence of the Setting Sun

In silence deep, the sun does set,
A tranquil hush, a calm duet.
The sky ignites in fiery glow,
As twilight dances, soft and slow.

Clouds embrace the fading light,
Whispers echo through the night.
Birds return to their warm nest,
In shadows deep, we find our rest.

When the Sky Dances with Darkness

When sky entwines with night's embrace,
A dance of shadows, a slow grace.
Stars emerge, their flicker bright,
As darkness paints the world in night.

Moonlight bathes the earth below,
Casting dreams in silver glow.
In the stillness, hearts will find,
A quiet peace, and love entwined.

Dusky Reverie

In twilight's soft embrace, shadows play,
Dreams unfurl like whispers of the day.
Stars begin to wink, a gentle tease,
Night's calm descends, a tender breeze.

The horizon blushes in fading light,
Birds hush their songs, surrender to night.
Each heartbeat echoes in tranquil air,
Lose oneself in visions, a soft snare.

A silence wraps the world in warm delight,
Fleeting moments blend in shades of night.
Memories linger like a soft caress,
In dusky dreams, we find our rest.

Misty thoughts drift like clouds in the sky,
Underneath the stars, our spirits fly.
Each sigh a promise, each glance a chance,
In this dusky reverie, we dance.

The Gradual Surrender of Day

As sun dips low, the skies start to glow,
Colors blend softly, a vibrant show.
The warmth of daylight retreats with grace,
Bidding farewell, to night's embrace.

Silhouettes gather on the horizon line,
Nature exhales, a moment divine.
The world transforms in hues deep and bold,
Stories of twilight patiently unfold.

Stars peek out, timid but bright,
Inviting us into the depths of night.
As shadows lengthen and merge with the ground,
In whispers of magic, we feel unbound.

The moon takes its throne in the starry dome,
Guiding lost souls, a place to roam.
The gradual surrender, a sweet refrain,
In every heartbeat, love's gentle gain.

Night's Gentle Arrival

When dusk wraps around in a velvet shawl,
Night's gentle arrival begins its call.
Crickets serenade the cool evening air,
Dreams gather close in the stillness so rare.

The moonlight dances on whispers of trees,
Breathing life into shadows that sway with ease.
Starlit tales weave through the fabric of night,
In quiet moments, we find our light.

Each heartbeat softens beneath the night's glow,
Minds can wander where wild thoughts flow.
Thoughts drift in silver, carried on streams,
In the art of night, we float on our dreams.

Embrace the silence, let worries release,
In night's gentle arms, we find our peace.
With every sigh, a journey begins,
In the calm of darkness, our spirit wins.

Veils of the Departing Sun

The sun bows low, hiding behind the hills,
Casting its gold with delicate thrills.
Veils of amber brush the evening sky,
A soft goodbye as daylight waves shy.

Clouds reflect the day's lingering glow,
Whispering secrets that only they know.
As colors bleed into a deepening blue,
Nature holds her breath, a world anew.

In the hush that follows, crickets begin,
Night awakens, inviting within.
By fading light, we release the day's thread,
In the calm twilight, our souls are fed.

With dawn yet to come, we find respite,
In the veils of dusk, so soft and light.
Each sunset glimmers as we softly sigh,
In the arms of night, we learn to fly.

Embers Against the Twilight

Flickers dance upon the night,
Whispers of the firelight.
Shadows stretch across the land,
Kissing dreams with gentle hand.

Stars awaken, one by one,
Guiding echoes of the sun.
As the sky turns deep and blue,
Embers flicker, old yet new.

Night enfolds the world in grace,
Holding time in warm embrace.
Yet the fire's fading glow
Keeps the heart from falling slow.

In the heart, memories gleam,
Like the remnants of a dream.
As twilight serenades the day,
Embers hint at love's ballet.

Softly Sinking

Whispers of the evening breeze,
Hold the sway of dancing trees.
Gentle waves on water's skin,
As the night begins to spin.

Moments linger, shadows blend,
In the twilight, time can bend.
All is wrapped in soft embrace,
Fading light in quiet grace.

Stars emerge with tender sighs,
Casting dreams across the skies.
Slowly drifting, hearts will find,
Peace in stillness, intertwined.

As the world begins to hush,
In this moment, feel the rush.
Softly sinking into night,
Wrapped in starlit, silver light.

An Evening's Benediction

As the sun dips low and whispers,
A soft prayer the twilight stirs.
Gold and crimson touch the sky,
Cradling dreams as they float by.

In the hush, a gentle call,
Nature's lullaby for all.
With each breath, the world aligns,
Gathering strength as daylight twines.

The moon ascends, a silver queen,
Casting spells on all unseen.
Beneath her gaze, a sacred trust,
In her glow, we linger, must.

Evening's gift, a sacred sigh,
Threads of night, where spirits fly.
In the calm, our hearts connect,
Finding peace, our souls reflect.

The Last Glow of Summer

In the garden, colors fade,
Whispers of the warmth we made.
Petals fall like drops of time,
Carried off in silent rhyme.

The breeze brings tales of the past,
Echoes of a season's cast.
As the sun dips low and sighs,
Days grow short beneath the skies.

Golden hues dapple the air,
Promises of coolness there.
Yet, in hearts, the warmth will stay,
Till the autumn calls its play.

In this moment, fleeting bliss,
Bathe in every sunset's kiss.
For as the last glow drifts away,
Summer's love will always stay.

Where Light Meets Its Rest

The sun dips low, a golden sphere,
Whispers of dusk begin to near.
Colors blend in warm embrace,
As shadows dance in twilight's grace.

The stars awaken, one by one,
A tapestry of night begun.
Moonlight spills on gentle land,
Where dreams are woven, hand in hand.

Reflections on the Horizon's Breath

Upon the waves, a shimmer plays,
Mirrored skies in evening's haze.
Gentle breezes softly sigh,
As day gives way to the night sky.

The horizon, a line so true,
Where colors blend in every hue.
Time wanders slow, in nature's trust,
And souls find peace in silver dust.

Lament of the Waning Light

As daylight fades, a quiet gloom,
The echoes hush in shadowed room.
A pang of loss in every breath,
The fading light, a quiet death.

Yet in the dark, new worlds take flight,
With glimmers of hope and dreams so bright.
Though shadows linger, hearts will mend,
For every end, there's light to send.

Celestial Farewells

In the sweep of cosmic night,
Stars bid farewell with gentle light.
Planets spin in graceful dance,
As time itself holds a fleeting glance.

Eclipsed by shadows, yet still they shine,
Guiding souls through space and time.
In each goodbye, new paths unfurl,
In the vast expanse of a wondrous world.

Twilight's Embrace

The sun dips low, a gentle sigh,
As colors blend in the evening sky.
Whispers of night begin to unfold,
Embracing the world in hues of gold.

Stars peek out, one by one,
The fading light, a day well done.
Night's velvet cloak drapes all around,
In twilight's arms, peace is found.

The moon ascends, a silver glare,
Softly lighting the shadows that dare.
Nature's hush breathes in the calm,
Wrapped in serenity like a balm.

Time slows down in twilight's grace,
A sacred pause, a warm embrace.
In this moment, all seems right,
As day gives way to the gentle night.

When Daylight Meets Nightfall

A golden orb begins to fade,
Casting shadows, memories made.
The sky ignites in blush and plume,
As stars awaken, dispelling gloom.

Birds retreat to nests so snug,
While breezes play a soothing tug.
The world holds breath, in stillness waits,
For night to open her quiet gates.

Crickets sing their lullabies,
Beneath the vast and starry skies.
The day concedes, a gentle rest,
In night's soft arms, we feel our best.

And as the twilight softly glows,
Our hearts align with nature's flows.
When daylight meets the evening call,
In this dance, we find our all.

Shadows of a Distant Sun

Fingers of light stretch far and wide,
Painting the world, a morn's proud stride.
Yet shadows linger, dark and deep,
Guarding secrets that lies keep.

Branches sway, casting nets of gloom,
While sunlight dares to chase the doom.
A dance of contrasts, bright and gray,
Echoes of stories from yesterday.

The sun sinks low, with grace and pride,
Leaving shadows where dreams reside.
In twilight's glow, they start to weave,
A tapestry of all we believe.

In every shadow, a tale resides,
Of laughter, sorrow, and all that hides.
As dusk descends and worlds collide,
We find ourselves on this shifting tide.

Secrets of the Setting Sky

Stormy clouds part, revealing light,
A canvas strokes the edge of night.
Crimson and indigo swirl in flight,
Secrets whisper as dark takes flight.

Each sunset brings a quiet thrill,
Promises linger, dreams to fulfill.
The horizon glows, a fleeting sign,
Of moments caught, forever mine.

As stars begin their nightly reign,
The setting sky reveals our pain.
Yet in the beauty, strength we find,
In shadows mingling, hearts entwined.

So pause awhile, let silence speak,
In twilight's heart, we're never weak.
For in the dusk, the truth applies,
In every ending, a new rise.

Where Day Meets Night

The sky blushes soft as the sun fades,
Shadows dance gently in twilight's embrace.
Whispers of dusk beckon the stars,
As day whispers secrets to night.

Moonlight draws curtains on day's bright show,
Crickets serenade in the cool evening air.
In the stillness, dreams begin to glow,
Where light and dark merge without a care.

Fleeting moments of time suspended,
As horizons blur, boundaries dissolve.
Here where the day and night are blended,
A tapestry of wonder is evolved.

Calmly the evening, tender and sweet,
Invites the stars to come take their place.
In the hush of night, hearts skip a beat,
In this sacred hour, we find grace.

Colors of the Setting Sun

Gold and crimson paint the open sky,
Clouds adorned in a fiery hue.
Nature's canvas bids the day goodbye,
Awakening dreams as night creeps through.

The horizon glimmers, a painter's delight,
With strokes of orange in a swirling dance.
Whispers of breezes serenade the night,
In the chills of dusk, we lose our chance.

Fields bask in warmth of the fading glow,
As shadows stretch long beneath the trees.
Nature's farewell, a soothing show,
Cradling the world in a gentle breeze.

Embrace the magic, let your soul unwind,
In the splendor of colors from above.
For within the twilight, peace we find,
A fleeting moment, a promise of love.

Beyond the Wane

Tides recede, whispers of the moon,
Echoes soft in the silver light.
Time lingers, old tunes find their tune,
In shadows deep, all comes to sight.

With every phase, a story unfolds,
Tales of change in the cool night air.
Stars align, destinies are told,
In the stillness, we find what's fair.

The waning crescent, a silent guide,
Leads us softly into the unknown.
Each gentle pulse, the heart's quiet stride,
Reminds us we're never alone.

Beyond the wane, a new dawn awaits,
Infinite wonders yet to be found.
Trust in the rhythm, open the gates,
Embrace the whispers, let love abound.

Cerulean Farewell

The sea waves bid with a cerulean heart,
Soft breezes carry a longing sigh.
Sunset curtains pull worlds apart,
As colors blend where the horizon lies.

Clouds hug the sky in shades of blue,
Kissing the waves with a gentle grace.
In this moment, dreams feel anew,
A fleeting look at a cherished place.

As daylight wanes, reflections shimmer,
On waters deep, where secrets flow.
Night calls softly, the stars grow dimmer,
The cerulean calm begins to glow.

Every farewell holds a promise bright,
Of tomorrow's journey, fresh and true.
In twilight's embrace, love's pure light,
Awaits the soul in every hue.

Milton Keynes UK
Ingram Content Group UK Ltd.
UKHW030751121124
451094UK00013B/777